LATIMER

BOOKS IN THIS SERIES

LATIMER

BAXTER

WHITEFIELD

—— J.C. RYLE ——

LATIMER

FOREWORD BY BENNETT W. ROGERS

H&E
Publishing

Latimer

All Scripture quotations are taken and adapted from the King James Version.

Published by: H&E Publishing, Peterborough, Canada
Editors: Chance Faulkner and Corey M.K. Hughes
Cover image original drawing: Hugh Latimer, 2018 Tyler Swaffield

Source in Public Domain: J.C. Ryle, *The Priest, the Puritan and the Preacher.* Published by New York: Robert Carter & Brothers, 1856.

Delivered before the young men's Christian association, in Exeter Hall, February 1st, 1853

First Edition, 2018
Printed in Canada

Paperback ISBN: 978-1-7752633-8-8
ePub ISBN: 978-1-989174-07-4

Contents

Series Introduction: Who Is J.C. Ryle ?..........vii
By Bennet W. Rogers

Foreword..xiii
By Bennet W. Rogers

Latimer

Introduction...1

1 Latimer's Times...5

2 Latimer's Life..21

3 Latimer's Opinions.....................................45

PUBLISHER'S NOTE

In this edition, the punctuation and capitalization have been modernized, some archaic words have been updated, and a few other slight editorial changes made.

ACKNOWLEDGMENTS

Thank you, Chidera Orji for your help transcribing this work. Thank you Benjamin Inglis and Ron Heyboer for your proofreading.

WHO IS J.C. RYLE (1816–1900)?

By Bennett W. Rogers

J.C. Ryle was born and raised in a wealthy but unspiritual home.[1] He distinguished himself academically and athletically at Eton and Oxford. He experienced an evangelical conversion in his final year at university, the account of which has achieved a semi-legendary status among evangelicals—a testimony to the power of the public reading of Scripture.[2] Shortly thereafter, his father's bankruptcy ruined the family, ended his political career before it started,

---

[1] For a life of Ryle, see Eric Russell, *J. C. Ryle: That Man of Granite with the Heart of a Child* (Fearn, Scotland: Christian Focus Publications, 2008); John Murray, Iain H. Murray, *J. C. Ryle: Prepared to Stand Alone* (Edinburgh, UK: Banner of Truth Trust, 2016); or my new intellectual biography of Ryle entitled *John Charles Ryle: The Man, His Ministry, and His Message* (Grand Rapids: Reformation Heritage Books, 2018).

[2] Around the time of his examinations, John Charles attended Carfax Church, formally known as St. Martin's, feeling somewhat depressed and discouraged. The reader of the lesson made some lengthy pauses when he came to verse 8: "By grace—are ye saved—through faith—and that, not of yourselves—it is the gift of God." This unusual and emphatic reading of Ephesians 2:8 made a tremendous impact on him and led to his own evangelical conversion.

and forced him into the ministry of the Church of England. Although he initially became a clergyman because he felt "shut up to it," Ryle quickly gained a reputation for being a powerful preacher, diligent pastor, popular author, and effective controversialist. He rose through the evangelical ranks to become the undisputed leader and party spokesman—the first to hold that distinction since Charles Simeon (1759-1836). He became the first Bishop of Liverpool in 1880 at an age (64) when many clergymen contemplate retirement, and served as the chief pastor of the second city of the British Empire until his death in 1900.

Ryle is probably best remembered as a writer of tracts, commentaries, and devotional works, and deservedly so. His tracts continue to be distributed. His commentaries on the gospels—*Expository Thoughts on the Gospels*—are still read by pastors and laymen alike. His practical writings, such as *Old Paths*, *Practical Religion*, and the *Upper Room* have remained popular with evangelical readers for well over a century. And *Holiness: Its Nature, Hindrances, Difficulties, and Roots* has become a modern spiritual classic. J. C. Ryle was also keenly interested in church history. In fact, he wrote twenty-five short biographies of important figures in English church history and published a number of popular historical works about the English Reformation.[3] Ryle believed that church

---

[3] Ryle wrote biographical sketches of the following persons: George Whitefield, John Wesley, William Grimshaw, William Romaine, Daniel Rowlands, John Berridge, Henry Venn, Samuel Walker, James Hervey, Augustus Toplady, Fletcher of Madeley, John Wycliffe, John Rogers,

history is not merely interesting—it is instructive. It is nothing less than "philosophy teaching by examples." And no period of church history was more instructive than the 16th, 17th, and 18th centuries.

At the beginning of the sixteenth century, Roman Catholicism reigned supreme, and as a result, the land was engulfed in darkness. The vast majority of the English people lived in a miserable state of spiritual ignorance, monstrous superstition, degrading priestcraft, and gross immorality. The Bible was outlawed. Divine worship was unintelligible. Essential Christian doctrine was lost. *Biblical* holiness was unknown. In short, "there was an utter famine of vital Christianity in the land."[4] The Protestant Reformation delivered England from all these evils. It gave Englishmen the Bible in their own language and permission to read it. It made religious worship simple, beautiful, and above all, intelligible. It revived the true teaching and preaching of the gospel, as well as the true standard of practical holiness. Ryle considered the Protestant Reformation of the sixteenth century to be the greatest blessing God ever bestowed on his country. And he regarded the martyred English Reformers,

---

John Hooper, Rowland Taylor, Hugh Latimer, John Bradford, Nicholas Ridley, Samuel Ward, Archbishop Laud, Richard Baxter, William Gurnall, James II and the Seven Bishops, Thomas Manton, and Colonel Robert Holden. For Ryle's works on the English Reformation see: *Lessons from English Church History*, *What Do We Owe the Reformation*, and *Why Were Our Reformers Burned*.

[4] J.C. Ryle, *Lessons from English Church History* (London: William Hunt and Company, 1871), 11.

like Bishop Hugh Latimer, to be the best churchmen who ever lived.

In the seventeenth century, a party led by Archbishop Laud, began to reverse the work of the reformation and un-protestantize the Church of England. These Laudian divines began to exalt the Supper, ceremonies, and the episcopacy, and disparage the Reformers, the Puritans, and Calvinism. The consequences of this departure from the principles of the Reformation was, in a word, disastrous. It alienated many Englishmen from the Church of England and essentially created English Dissent. It led to a bloody civil war and the temporary destruction of the Church of England. And after the Restoration and the passage of the Act of Uniformity, it forced out two thousand of England's most able and holy ministers in the Great Ejection, including the famous pastor of Kidderminster, Richard Baxter.

In the years that followed, English Christianity began to die a slow death. Natural theology, cold morality, and barren orthodoxy took root in Church and chapel. Infidelity and skepticism became popular, even fashionable. The bishops and clergy of the Church of England were worldly and ineffective. The Nonconformists won their religious liberty but lost their religious zeal. Immorality—dueling, drunkenness, and adultery—abounded. And the evangelical activism that would characterize that closing decades of the eighteenth century were nonexistent. But in the midcentury English Christianity was rescued and revived by the evangelical revival. The leaders of this Great Awakening, like

George Whitefield, turned the nation upside down through their preaching and evangelism. They proclaimed the doctrine of the Puritans and the Reformers simply, fervently, and ubiquitously, and as a result, English Christianity was saved from the brink.

Hugh Latimer, Richard Baxter, and George Whitefield represent the best men and ministers of their respective ages. They show us what great influence one man can have on his generation when he has the truth on his side. J. C. Ryle was convinced that the Church of his day needed more bishops like Latimer, more pastors like Baxter, and more preachers like Whitefield. Though more than 160 years have passed since Ryle first published these biographical sketches, the need for such men remains unchanged. May these biographies inspire a new generation of Latimers, Baxters, and Whitefields.

FOREWORD

By Bennett W. Rogers

This short biography of the martyred bishop and reformer, Hugh Latimer, was one of Ryle's first historical works. It was originally a lecture delivered before the Church of England's Young Men's Society for Aiding Missions at Home and Abroad.[5] Due to its popularity, Ryle's publisher, William Hunt, published it along with similar biographical sketches of Richard Baxter and George Whitefield in *The Bishop, the Pastor, and the Preacher* in 1854. It would be republished throughout Ryle's lifetime and beyond.

Ryle examines the ministry of Bishop Latimer under three headings: 1) Latimer's times; 2) Latimer's life; 3) Latimer's opinions. These are the aspects of Latimer's

---

[5] The Church of England's Young Mens' Society, as it was later called, was founded in 1844 for the moral, intellectual, and spiritual improvement of young churchmen; to cultivate the missionary spirit; and to collect funds for the Church Pastoral Aid Society, the Colonial Church and School Society, the London Society for Promoting Christianity Amongst the Jews, and the Church Missionary Society. For a brief overview of this society, its work, and this volume see *The Christian Observer*, 175 July 1852, 477–485.

history that Ryle found most instructive. When Ryle first delivered this lecture, a group of churchmen were actively seeking to un-Protestantize the Church of England and bring it closer to the Church of Rome in both worship and doctrine. Ryle became the leading Evangelical opponent of this new movement, called Ritualism, in the 1860's and 1870's and assailed it through every means available to him: the pulpit, lectern, platform, and the press. Ryle's lecture on Latimer spoke directly to this emerging threat in the early 1850's. Latimer's *times*, which were characterized by gross spiritual and moral darkness, as well as tyrannical persecution, reveal the true fruits of Popery. Latimer's religious *opinions*, which are enshrined in the Church's *Homilies*, as well as in his writings, reveal what one of the founders, bishops, Reformers, and martyrs of the Church of England thought were "church views."

There is much more here, however, than anti-Ritualist polemics. Latimer's *life* is an example to all Christians. He is an example to all Christian ministers. Ryle considered him to be one of the finest bishops the Church of England has ever had. In his mind, Latimer was the prototypical "Reforming Bishop." In 1880 Ryle would become the first Bishop of the Second City of the British Empire, and those who are familiar with his episcopacy will note that his reforming agenda for Liverpool was strikingly similar to Latimer's in Worcester. Latimer is also a model for all Christians more generally. He shows us what tremendous influence one Christian can have on his generation. Ryle believed that Christians of Latimer's stamp were desperately needed in his own generation. They are needed in every generation.

There is even more in this biographical sketch to commend this new edition of Ryle's famous lecture to a new generation of readers. Latimer's conversion, as well as his martyrdom, are deeply moving. The judicious use of quotations gives the reader a taste of Latimer's boldness and conviction, as well as his outspoken Protestantism. And Ryle's characteristic simplicity and directness makes *Latimer* an easy and edifying read for all Christians. I highly commend this new edition!

INTRODUCTION

I have no doubt the name of Bishop Latimer is known to
almost all who read this book.[6] There are probably few who
have forgotten that three hundred years ago there was such a
queen of England as bloody Mary, and that men were burned
alive in her reign because they would not desert Christ's
truth—and that one of these men was Bishop Latimer.

But I want young Englishmen to know these things better.
I want them to become thoroughly familiar with the lives, the
acts, and the opinions of the leading English Reformers.
Their names ought to be something better than hackneyed
ornaments to point a platform speech, and rhetorical traps to
elicit an Exeter Hall[7] cheer. Their principles ought no longer
to be vague, hazy shadows, "looming in the distance," but
something clear, distinct, and well-defined before your
mind's eyes. My desire is that you may understand that the
best interests of this country are bound up with Protestantism.

---

[6] Original: all who are here tonight.
[7] J.C Ryle is delivering this lecture at Exeter Hall before the Church
of England's Young Men's Society.

My wish is that you may write on your hearts that the wellbeing of England depends not on commerce, or politics, or steam, or armies, or navies, or gold, or corn but on the maintenance of the principles of the English Reformation.

The times you live in call loudly for the diffusion of knowledge about English Church history. Opinions are boldly broached nowadays of so startling a nature, that they make a man rub his eyes, and say, "Where am I?" A state of feeling is growing up among us about Romanism and Protestantism which, to say the least, is most unhealthy. It has increased, is increasing, and ought to be diminished. Nothing is so likely to check this state of feeling as the production of a few plain facts. If you want to convince a Scotchman, they say, you must give him a long argument. If you want to convince an Englishman, you must give him plain facts. Facts are the principal commodity I have brought here in this work.[8] If anyone desires[9] private speculations, or oratorical display, I am afraid he will go away disappointed; but if anyone likes plain facts, I think I shall be able to supply him with a few.

Are any of you in doubt who is a true member of the Church of England? Are you perplexed by the rise and progress of what are foolishly called "Church views?" Come with me in this book,[10] and pay a visit to one of the Fathers of the English Church. Let us put into the witness-box one of the most honest and outspoken bishops of the days of the

---

[8] Original: here tonight.
[9] Original: anyone has come to hear.
[10] Original: me tonight.

English Reformation. Let us examine the life and opinions of good old Latimer.

Are any of you doubting what is the true character of the Church of Rome? Are you bewildered by some of those plausible gentlemen who tell you there is no fundamental difference between the Anglican and Romish Churches? Are you puzzled by that intense yearning after so-called Catholic principles which distinguishes some misguided church men, and which exhibits itself in Catholic teaching, Catholic ceremonies, Catholic books of devotion, and Catholic architecture? Come with me,[11] and turn over a few old pages in English history. Let us see what England actually was when Romish teachers instructed the English people, and had things all their own way. Let us see what the Church of Rome does when she has complete power. Let us see how she treats the friends of an open Bible, of private judgment, and of justification by faith. Let us see how the Church of Rome dealt with Bishop Latimer.

And now, without further preface, let me try to tell you something about:

1. Latimer's times.
2. Latimer's life.
3. Latimer's opinions.

---

[11] Original: come with me tonight.

1
LATIMER'S TIMES

The times of Bishop Latimer deserve attentive consideration. It is impossible to form a just estimate of a man's conduct unless we know the circumstances in which he is placed, and the difficulties with which he has to contend. No one is thoroughly aware of the extent of our obligations to the noble band of English Reformers who is not acquainted with the actual state of England when they began their work, and the amazing disadvantages under which their work was carried on.

Latimer was born in the reign of Henry VII. He lived through the reigns of Henry VIII and Edward VI and was put to death in the reign of Queen Mary.[12] He began life at a period when Popery[13] bore undisputed sway in this country. He witnessed the beginning of the breach between Henry VII and Rome, and the establishment of a transition state of

---

[12] Born circa 1485 during the reign of King Henry VII (1485–1509). Lived through the reign of Henry VIII (1509–1547), Edward VI (1547–1553) and died during the reign of "Bloody" Queen Mary (1553–1558) specifically on October 16, 1555. – C.H.

[13] *Popery* meaning the practices or teachings relating to the Pope or papacy in Roman Catholicism.

religion in England. He lived to see the full development of Protestantism under Edward VI, and the compilation of a Liturgy and Articles very slightly differing from those we have at this day. Of each of these three periods I must say a few words.

When Popery was supreme

The period of Latimer's life when Popery was supreme in England, was a period of utter spiritual darkness. The depth of superstition in which our worthy forefathers were sunk is enough to make one's hair stand on end. No doubt there were many Lollards, and followers of Wycliffe, scattered over the land who held the truth and were the salt of the nation. But the fierce persecution with which these good men were generally assailed prevented their making much progress. They barely maintained their own ground. And as for the mass of the population, gross darkness covered their minds.

Most of the priests and teachers of religion were themselves profoundly ignorant of everything they ought to have known. They were generally ordained without any adequate examination as to learning or character. Many of them, though they could read their breviaries,[14] knew nothing whatever of the Bible. Some, according to Strype[15] the historian, were scarcely able to say the Lord's prayer, and not a few were unable to repeat the ten commandments. The

---

[14] *Breviaries* meaning a book containing psalms, hymns, prayers.
[15] John Strype (1643–1737).

prayers of the Church were in the Latin language, which hardly anybody understood. There was scarcely any preaching, and what there was, was grossly unscriptural and unedifying.[16] Quarterly sermons were prescribed to the clergy, but not insisted on. Mass, according to Latimer, was not to be omitted for a single Sunday but sermons might be omitted for twenty Sundays together, and nobody found fault.

Huge nests of ordained men were dotted over the face of England in the shape of abbeys and monasteries. The inhabitants of these beautiful buildings were seldom very holy and self-denying, and were often men of most profligate and disreputable lives. Their morals were just what might have been expected from fullness of bread and abundance of idleness. They did next to nothing for the advancement of learning. They did nothing for the spread of true religion. Two things only they cared for and those two were to fill their own pockets, and to keep up their own power. For the one purpose they persuaded weak and dying people to give money and land to the Church, under the specious pretense that they would in this way be delivered from purgatory, and their faith proved by their good works. For the other purpose they claimed to hold the keys of the kingdom of heaven. To them confession of sins must be made. Without their absolution and extreme unction no man could be saved. Without their masses, no soul could be redeemed from purgatory. In short,

---

[16] Original: Preaching there was scarcely any, and what there was, was grossly unscriptural.

they were practically the mediators between Christ and man, and to injure them was the highest offense and sin. Old Fuller tells us, for example, that in 1489, a certain Italian got an immense sum of money in England by:

> having power from the Pope to absolve people from usury, simony, theft, manslaughter, fornication, and adultery, and all crimes whatsoever, except smiting the clergy, and conspiring against the Pope.[17]

Such were Romish priests in Latimer's youth, when Popery was last rampant in England. To say that they were generally ignorant, covetous, sensual, and despotic tyrants over the souls and bodies of men, is not saying one jot more than the truth.

When priests in Latimer's youth were men of this stamp, you will not be surprised to hear that the people were utterly ignorant of true religion. It would have been miraculous indeed if it had been otherwise, when they had neither sound preaching to hear nor Bibles to read. A New Testament could not be bought for less than £3.00,[18] and the buyer was in danger of being considered a heretic for purchasing it. The Christianity of the vast majority was, naturally enough, a mere name and form. The Sabbath was a day of sport and pastime, and not a day of solemn worship. Not one in a hundred, perhaps, could have rightly answered the question,

---

[17] Thomas Fuller, *The Church History of Britain*, I, 533.
[18] Original: 2l. 16s. 3d (2 pounds, 16 shillings, 3 pence).

"What shall I do to be saved?" or given the slightest account of justification, regeneration, sanctification, the office of Christ, or the work of the Spirit. A man's only idea of the way to heaven generally was to do as the priest told him and to belong to the true Church. Thus the blind led the blind, and all wallowed in the ditch together.

All the practical religion that the mass of the laity possessed, consisted in prayers to the Virgin and saints— pilgrimages to holy places—and adoration of images and relics. The list of their superstitious practices would make an appalling catalogue. They hastened to the church for holy water before a thunderstorm. They resorted to St. Rooke in times of pestilence. They prayed to St. Pernal in an ague.[19] Young women, desiring to be married, sought the help of St. Nicholas. Wives, weary of their husbands, betook themselves to St. Uncumber. One hundred thousand pilgrims visited the tomb of St. Thomas à Becket at Canterbury in one year in order to help their souls toward heaven. In one year, at Canterbury Cathedral, there was offered at Christ's altar, more than £3.00[20] on the Virgin Mary's, over £63.00[21] and on Thomas à Becket's, over £832.00.[22]

The images worshiped were often gross cheats as well as idols. At Bexley, in Kent, there was a famous crucifix on which the figure of our Lord would move its head, hands, and

---

[19] *Ague* meaning an illness involving fever and shivering.
[20] Original: 3l. 2s. 6d. (3 pounds, 2 shillings, 6 pence).
[21] Original: 63l. 5s. 6d. (63 pounds, 5 shillings, 6 pence).
[22] Original: 832l. 12s. 3d (832 pounds, 12 shillings, 3 pence).

feet, roll its eyes, move its lips, and bend its brow. It would hang its lips when silver was offered to it, and shake its head merrily when the offering was gold. And all this was thought miraculous. At length it was discovered that the image was full of springs and wires, and that the movements were caused by priests or their agents secreted near it. The relics worshiped were as monstrous and absurd as the images. At Hales, in Gloucestershire, there was shown in a crystal vial,[23] what was called the blood of Christ, but it was at length discovered to be the blood of a duck. At Reading, there was shown an angel with one wing, who brought over the spear that pierced our Lord's side. At Bury, in Suffolk, the coals that roasted St. Lawrence, the pairings of St. Edmond's toe-nails, and St. Thomas à Becket's penknife and boots, were all religiously adored. As to wood of the true Cross, enough was found in the churches, when relics were finally cast out, to have made two or three crosses. As to the bones of saints, there were whole heaps which had been venerated for years which proved at length to be bones of pigs. These are dreadful things to tell, but they ought to be known. All these things the Church of Rome knew, connived at, sanctioned, defended, taught, and enforced on her members. This was the state of religion in England in the 16th Century,[24] when the English Reformers were raised up. This was English Christianity in the childhood and youth of Hugh Latimer.

---

[23] Original: a crystal phial.
[24] Original: England three hundred and fifty years ago.

Transition between Romanism and Protestantism

The second period of Latimer's life, during which England was in a state of transition between Romanism and Protestantism, presents many curious features.

We see on the one hand, a reformation of religion begun by a king from motives which, to say the least, were not spiritual. It would be absurd to suppose that a sensual tyrant like Henry VIII came to a breach with the Pope for any other reason than that the Pope crossed his will. We see his pretended scruples about his marriage with Catharine of Arragon bringing him into communication with Cranmer and Latimer. We see him at one time so far guided by the advice of these good men that, like Herod, he does many things that are right, and calculated to advance the cause of the Gospel. He makes Cranmer Archbishop of Canterbury[25] and shows him favour to the very end of his days. He allows the Bible to be printed in English, and placed in churches. He commands images to be broken, and puts down many gross superstitions. He boldly denies the doctrine of the Pope's supremacy. He dissolves the monasteries, and puts to open shame the wickedness of their inmates. All this we see, and are thankful.

We see him at another time defending Popish dogmas and burning men who, like the martyr Lambert, denied them. We see him putting forth the famous Six Articles, which re-asserted transubstantiation, private masses, clerical celibacy, vows of chastity, auricular confession, and the denial of the

---

[25] Thomas Cranmer (1489–1556).

cup to the laity. Worst of all, we see in him the marks of a proud, self-willed, sensual man all his life long, and an utter want of evidence that his heart was ever right in the sight of God. The use of a man who was guilty of such inconsistencies, to do God's work is among the deep things of God's providence. We cannot understand it. We must wait.

Turning on the other hand from Henry VIII to the first English Reformers, we see in them strong indications of what Fuller calls "a twilight religion." We see them putting forth books in Henry VIII's reign, which, though an immense improvement and advance upon Romish teaching, still contain some things which are not Scriptural. Such were the "necessary erudition," and the "institution of a Christian man." We see them, however, gradually growing in spiritual knowledge, perhaps unaware to themselves, and specially as to the error of transubstantiation. We see them continually checked and kept back, partly by the arbitrary conduct of the king, partly by the immense difficulty of working side by side with a Popish party in the church, and partly by the great ignorance of the parochial clergy. Nevertheless, on comparing the end of Henry VIII's reign with the beginning, we see plain proof that much ground was gained. We learn to admire the overruling power of God, who can use a Henry VIII just as he did a Nebuchadnezzar or Sennacherib, for the accomplishment of His own purposes.

The patient perseverance of the Reformers

And last but not least, we learn to admire the patient perseverance of the Reformers. Though they had but a little strength they used it. Though they had but a small door open, they entered in by it. Though they had but one talent, they laid it out heartily for God, and did not bury it in the ground. Though they had but a little light, they lived fully up to it. If they could not do what they would, they did what they could, and were blessed in their deed. Such was the second period of Latimer's life. Never let it be forgotten that, at that time, the foundations of the Church of England were excavated, and vast heaps of rubbish removed out of the way of the builders who were to follow. Viewed in this light, it will always be an interesting period to the student of church history.

The reign of Edward VI

The last period of Latimer's life, which comprises the reign of Edward VI is in many respects very different from the two periods to which I have already averted. The cause of English Protestantism made immense progress during Edward's short but remarkable tenure of power. It was truly said of him by Hooker, that "he died young, but lived long, if life be action." Released from the bondage of a tyrannical king's interference, Cranmer and his friends went forward in the work of religious reformation with rapid strides. Bonner and Gardiner were no longer allowed to keep them back. Refusing to take part in the good work, these two Popish prelates were deposed and put to silence. Faithful men, like Ridley and

Hooper, were placed on the episcopal bench. An immense clearance of Popish ceremonies was effected. A Liturgy was compiled, which differed very slightly from our present Prayer-Book. The forty-two articles of religion were drawn up which form the basis of our own thirty-nine. The first book of Homilies was put forth, in order to supply the want of preachers. An accuracy and clearness of doctrinal statement was arrived at, which had until now been unknown. Learned foreigners, like Bucer and Peter Martyr, were invited to visit England, and appointed Regius Professors of Divinity at Oxford and Cambridge. How much further the Reformers might have carried the work of reformation if they had had time; it is useless now to speculate. Judging by the changes they effected in a very few years, they would probably have made our church as nearly perfect as a visible Church can be, if they had not been stopped by Edward's premature death.

There was however one thing which the Reformers of Edward the Sixth's reign could not accomplish. They could not change the hearts of the parochial clergy. Thousands of clergymen continued to hold office in the church of England who had no sympathy with the proceedings of Cranmer and his party. There was no getting rid of these worthies, for they were ready to promise anything, sign anything, swear anything, in order to keep their livings. But while they yielded compliance to Cranmer's injunctions and commands, they were graceless, ignorant, and semi-Papists at heart. The questions which Bishop Hooper found it necessary to put to the dean, prebendaries,[26] and clergy of the diocese of Gloucester on his first visitation, furnish us with a sad illustration of the state of English clergymen in Edward the Sixth's time. They are as follows:

> How many commandments are there? Where are they written? Can you say them by heart? What are the articles of the Christian faith? Can you repeat them? Can you confirm them by Scripture? Can you recite the Lord's prayer? How do you know it to be the Lord's prayer? Where is it written?[27]

These questions are sad enough, but what will you think of the result of the inquiry? Out of three hundred and eleven clergymen in the diocese of Gloucester, it turned out that one hundred and sixty-eight could not repeat the ten commandments, and out of these thirty-one could not state in what part of the Scriptures they were to be found. Forty of the three hundred and eleven could not tell where the Lord's prayer was written, and thirty-one did not know who was its Author.

Facts such as these are painful and astounding but it is most important that you should know them. They explain at once the ease with which bloody Mary restored Popery when she came to the throne. Parochial clergymen like those just described were not likely to offer any resistance to her wishes.

---

[26] *Prebendary* meaning a senior member of clergy, normally supported by the revenues from an estate or parish.
[27] *The Works of John Hooper*, II, 151.

Facts such as these throw great light on the position of Cranmer, and the Reformers of Edward the Sixth's days. We probably have little idea of the immense difficulties, both within and without, which beset them. Above all, facts such as these give you some idea of the condition of religion in England even in the brightest portion of Latimer's times. If things like these were to be seen when Latimer was an old man, what must have been seen when he was young? If ignorance like this prevailed under Edward VI, how thick must the darkness have been under Henry VIII!

I must dwell no longer on the subject of Latimer's times. I fear that I shall have wearied you already with a dry and tedious detail of facts. But I firmly believe that a knowledge of these facts is absolutely essential to a right understanding of the English Reformation and I therefore hope they will not prove useless.

On calm consideration, I trust you will agree with me that it is the height of absurdity to say, as some do nowadays, that this country has been a loser by getting rid of Popery. It is really astonishing to hear the nonsense talked "about merry England in the olden times," the "mediaeval piety," the "ages of faith," and the "devout habits of our Catholic forefathers."

Walter Scott's beautiful writings, and Pugin's beautiful architectural designs have lent a false glare to Romanism in England, and induced many to doubt whether our Reformation really was a gain. I do trust that young London will not be so young as to listen to such delusive theories.

Doubt not for a moment that the state of English society which Scott has sometimes made so beautiful by his pen, and Pugin by his pencil, is a far more beautiful thing in poems and pictures than it ever was in honest reality. Depend upon it, that "distance lends enchantment to the view." Rest satisfied, that Netley, and Glastonbury, and Tintern, and Bury, and Fountains, and Melrose, and Bolton Abbeys, are probably more useful now in ruins than ever they were in Henry the Seventh's days. Never forget what we have gained by the Reformation—we have gained light, knowledge, morality, and religious liberty. Never forget the fruits which grew on the tree of Popery when last it flourished in England. These fruits were ignorance, superstition, immorality, and priestly tyranny. God was angered. Souls were lost, and the devil was pleased.

Again, I trust you will feel with me in this moment[28] that it is most unfair to suppose that the acts and writings of the English Reformers under Henry VIII are any real criterion of their matured opinions. It is as unfair as it would be to measure the character of a grown-up man by his sayings and doings when he was a child. Remember that the Reformers under Henry VIII were in a state of spiritual childhood. They saw many points in religion through a glass darkly. It was not till the reign of Edward VI that they put away childish things. Beware therefore, lest any man ever deceive you by artfully chosen quotations drawn from works published in the

---

[28] Original: me tonight.

17

beginning of the English Reformation. Judge the Reformers, if you will, by their writings in the reign of Edward VI but not by their writings in the reign of Henry VIII.

Lastly, I trust that you will agree with me,[29] that it is most unreasonable to decry the early English Reformers as men who did not go far enough. Such charges are easily made but those who make them seldom consider the enormous obstacles the Reformers had to surmount, and the enormous evils they had to remove. It is nonsense to suppose they had nothing more to do than to pare the moss off an old building, and whitewash it afresh. They had to take down an old decayed house, and rebuild it from the very ground. It is nonsense to talk as if they had a smooth sea, a fair wind, and a clear course. On the contrary, they had to pilot the ship of true religion through a narrow and difficult strait, against current, wind, and tide. Put all their difficulties together—the arbitrary, profligate character of Henry VIII and the tender years of Edward VI, the general ignorance of the population, the bitter enmity of dispossessed monks and friars, the open opposition of many of the bishops, and the secret indifference of a vast proportion of the clergy—put all these things together, and weigh them well, and then I think you will not lightly regard the work that the early Reformers did. For my own part, so far from wondering that they did so little, I wonder rather that they did so much. I marvel at their firmness. I am surprised at their success. I see immense

---

[29] Original: me tonight.

results produced by comparatively weak instruments, and I can only account for it by saying, that "God was with them of a truth."[30]

---

[30] Original included this final paragraph: The second part of this evening's lecture, to which I shall next invite your attention, is the story of Bishop Latimer's life.

2

LATIMER'S LIFE

Early Life

Hugh Latimer was born about the year 1485, at Thurcaston, near Mount Sorrel, in the county of Leicester. He has left such a graphic account of his father and family in one of his sermons, preached before Edward VI, that I must in justice give it to you in his own words. He says:

> My father was a yeoman,[31] and had no lands of his own. He had only a farm of three or four pounds a year at the uttermost, and hereupon he tilled so much as kept half a dozen men. He had to walk for one hundred sheep, and my mother milked thirty cows.[32] He was able, and did bring the king a harness with himself and his horse, when he came to the place where he should receive the king's wages. I can remember that I buckled his harness when he went to Blackheath field. He kept me to school, or else I had not been able to have preached before the

---

[31] *Yeoman* is a man holding and cultivating a small landed estate.
[32] Original: kine.

king's majesty now. He married my sisters with five pounds apiece, and brought them up in godliness and the fear of God. He kept hospitality for his poor neighbors, and some alms he gave to the poor.[33]

Such is the good bishop's homely account of his own family. It is only fair to observe that Latimer is one among the thousand examples on record that England, with all its faults, is a country where a man may begin very low, and yet live to rise very high.

Life as a Papist

Latimer was sent to Cambridge at the age of fourteen, and in 1509 was elected a fellow of Clare Hall. We know very little of his early history, except the remarkable fact which he himself has told us, that up to the age of thirty he was a most violent and bigoted Papist. Just as St. Paul was not ashamed to tell men that at one time he was a blasphemer, a persecutor, and injurious, so the old Protestant bishop used often to tell how he too had once been the slave of Rome. He says in one of his sermons:

> I was as obstinate a Papist as any was in England, insomuch that when I should be made a bachelor of divinity, my whole oration went against Philip Melancthon and his opinions.[34]

---

[33] *The Works of Hugh Latimer*, I, 101.
[34] Latimer, *Works*, I, 334.

He says, in another sermon:

> All the Papists think themselves to be saved by the law, and I myself was of that dangerous, perilous, and damnable opinion till I was thirty years of age. So long had I walked in darkness and the shadow of death.[35]

He says, in a letter to Sir Edward Baynton:

> I have thought in times past that if I had been a friar, and in a cowl, I could not have been damned, nor afraid of death; and by reason of the same, I have been minded many times to have been a friar, namely, when I was sore sick, or diseased. Now I abhor my superstitious foolishness.[36]

Latimer's testimony about himself is confirmed by others. It is recorded that he used to think so ill of the Reformers, that he declared the last times, the Day of Judgment, and the end of the world must be approaching. "Impiety," he said, "was gaining ground apace, and what lengths might not men be expected to run, when they began to question even the infallibility of the Pope." Becon mentions, that when Stafford, the divinity lecturer, delivered lectures on the Bible, Latimer was sure to be present, in order to frighten and drive away the scholars. In fact, his zeal for Popery was so notorious, that he was elected to the office of cross-bearer in the religious

---

[35] Latimer, *Works,* I, 187.
[36] Latimer, *Works,* I, 332.

processions of the University, and discharged the duty with becoming solemnity for seven years. Such was the clay of which God formed a precious vessel ready for his work. Such were the first beginnings of one of the best and most useful of the English Reformers.

Conversion

The instrument which God used in order to bring this furious Papist to a knowledge of Christ's truth, was a student named Bilney. Bilney was a contemporary of Latimer's at Cambridge, who had for some time embraced the doctrines of the Reformation. He perceived that Latimer was a sincere and honest man, and kindly thought it possible that his zeal for Popery might arise from a lack of knowledge. He therefore went boldly to him after his public onslaught on Melanchthon, and humbly asked to be allowed to make a private confession of his own faith. The success of this courageous step was complete. Old Latimer tells us:

> I learned more by his confession than before in many years. From that time forward I began to smell the Word of God, and forsook the school-doctors, and such fooleries.[37]

Bilney's conduct on this occasion seems to have been most praiseworthy. It ought to encourage everyone to try to do good to his neighbor. It is a shining proof of the truth of

---

[37] Latimer, *Works*, I, 335.

the proverb, "A word spoken in season, how good is it" (Prov. 15:23).

Hugh Latimer was not a man to do anything by halves. As soon as he ceased to be a zealous Papist, he began at once to be a zealous Protestant, and gave himself up, body, soul, and mind, to the work of doing good. He visited, in Bilney's company, the sick and prisoners. He commenced preaching in the university pulpits, in a style which until then was unknown in Cambridge,[38] and soon became famous as one of the most striking and powerful preachers of the day. He stirred up hundreds of his hearers to search the Scriptures, and inquire after the way of salvation. Becon, afterward chaplain to Cranmer, and Bradford, afterward chaplain to Ridley, both traced their conversion to his sermons. Becon has left us a remarkable description of the effects of his preaching. He says:

> None, except the stiff-necked and uncircumcised in heart, went away from it without being affected with high detestation of sin, and moved unto all godliness and virtue.[39]

Opposition

The consequences of this faithful discharge of ministerial duty were just what all experience might lead us to expect. There arose against Latimer a storm of persecution. Swarms

---

[38] Original: a style hitherto unknown.
[39] Latimer, *Works,* II, 224.

of friars and doctors who had admired him when he carried the cross as a Papist, rose up against him in a body, when he preached the cross like St. Paul. The Bishop of Ely forbade his preaching any more in the university pulpits and had he not obtained permission from Dr. Barnes to preach in the church of the Augustine Friars, which was exempt from Episcopal jurisdiction, he might have been silenced altogether. But the malice of his enemies did not stop here. Complaints were laid against him before Cardinal Wolsey, and he had more than once to appear before him, and Tonstall, Bishop of London, on charges of heresy. Indeed, when the circumstances of the times are considered, it is wonderful that Latimer did not at this period of his life share Bilney's fate, and suffer death at the stake.

But the Lord, in whose hands our times are, had more work for Latimer to do, and raised up for him unexpected friends in higher quarters. His decided opinions in favour of Henry the Eighth's divorce from Catherine of Arragon, brought him into communication with Dr. Butts, the king's physician, and ultimately secured him the favour and patronage of the king himself. In the year 1530, he was made one of the royal chaplains, and preached before the king several times. In the year 1531, the royal favour procured for him an appointment to the living of West Kington, near Chippenham, in Wiltshire and, in spite of his friend Dr. Butts' remonstrances, he at once left court, and went to reside upon his cure.

At West Kington, Latimer was just the same man that he had been while he was most recently[40] at Cambridge, and found the devil just as busy an adversary in Wiltshire, as he had found him in the University. In pastoral labors he was abundant. In preaching he was instant in season and out of season, both within his parish and without. This he had full authority to do, by virtue of a general license from the University of Cambridge. But the more he did, the angrier the idle Popish clergy round West Kington became, and the more they labored to stop his proceedings. So true is it that human nature is the same in all ages. There is generally a dog-in-the-manger spirit about a graceless minister. He neither does good himself, nor likes anyone else to do it for him. This was the case with the Pharisees: they "took away the key of knowledge: they entered not in themselves, and them that were entering in they hindered" (Luke 11:52). And as it was in the days of the Pharisees, so it was in the days of Latimer.

On one occasion, the mayor and magistrates of Bristol, who were very friendly to him, had appointed him to preach before them on Easter day. Public notice had been given, and everybody was looking forward to the sermon with pleasure, for Latimer was very popular in Bristol. Suddenly there came out an order from the bishop, forbidding any one to preach in Bristol without his license. The clergy of the place waited on Latimer, and informed him of the bishop's order, and then, knowing well that he had no such license, told him "that they

---

[40] Original: been latterly at Cambridge.

were extremely sorry they were deprived of the pleasure of hearing an excellent discourse from him." Their compliments and crocodile regrets were unfortunately, ill-timed. Latimer had heard the whole history of the affair. And he knew well that these smooth-tongued gentlemen were the very persons who had written to the bishop in order to prevent his preaching.

For four years, while vicar of West Kington, the good man was subjected to a constant succession of petty worrying attacks and attempts to stop him from doing good. He was cited to London, and brought before Archbishop Warham, and detained many months from home. He was convened before convocation, and excommunicated and imprisoned for a time. But the protecting care of God seems to have been always round him. His enemies appear to have been marvelously restrained from carrying their malice to extremities.

Promotion to Bishop

At length, in 1535, the king put a sudden stop to their persecution by making him Bishop of Worcester. That such a man should make such an appointment, is certainly very wonderful. Some have attributed it to the influence of Lord Cromwell; some to that of Queen Anne Boleyn; some to that of Dr. Butts; some to that of Cranmer, who was always Latimer's fast friend. Such speculations are, to say the best, useless. "The king's heart is in the hand of the Lord: as the rivers of the south, he turns it whithersoever he will" (Prov.

21:1). When God intends to give a good man a high office, he can always raise up a Darius to convey it to him.

The history of Latimer's episcopate is short and simple, for it only lasted four years. He was the same man in a bishop's palace, that he had been in a country parsonage, or a Cambridge pulpit. Promotion did not spoil him. The miter did not prove an extinguisher to his zeal for the Gospel. He was always faithful, always simple-minded, always about his Father's business, always laboring to do good to souls. Foxe, the historian, speaks highly of:

> his pains, study, readiness, and continual carefulness in teaching, preaching, exhorting, visiting, correcting, and reforming, either as his ability could serve, or the times would bear.[41]

But he adds,

> the days then were so dangerous and variable that he could not in all things do what he would. Yet what he might do, that he performed to the uttermost of his strength, so that, although he could not utterly extinguish all the sparkling relics of old superstition, yet he so wrought that though they could not be taken away, yet they should be used with as little hurt, and as much profit as might be.[42]

---

[41] John Foxe, *Fox's Book of Martyrs: The Acts and Monuments of the Church*, III, (London: G. Virtue, 1844), 434.

[42] *Fox's Book of Martyrs*, 434.

In 1536, we find Bishop Latimer appointed by
Archbishop Cranmer to preach before the convocation of the
clergy. No doubt this appointment was made advisedly.
Cranmer knew well that Latimer was just the man for the
occasion. The sermons he preached are still extant, and fully
justify the archbishop's choice. Two more faithful and
conscience-stirring discourses were probably never delivered
to a body of ordained men. They will repay an attentive
perusal:

> Good brethren and fathers, seeing we are here
> assembled for the love of God, let us do something
> whereby we may be known to be the children of light.
> Let us do somewhat, lest we, which formerly have
> been judged children of the world, prove even still to
> be so. All men call us prelates; then, seeing we be in
> council, let us so order ourselves that we be prelates
> in honor and dignity, that we may be prelates in
> holiness, benevolence, diligence, and sincerity.[43]

> Lift up your heads, brethren, and look about with
> your eyes, and spy what things are to be reformed in
> the Church of England. Is it so hard, so great a
> matter, for you to see many abuses in the clergy, and
> many in the laity?[44]

He then mentions several glaring abuses by name: the
state of the Court of Arches and the Bishop's Consistories,

[43] Latimer, *Works,* I, 51.
[44] Latimer, *Works,* I, 52.

the number of superstitious ceremonies and holidays, the worship of images and visiting of relics and saints, the lying miracles and the sale of masses, and calls upon them to consider and amend them. He winds up all by a solemn warning of the consequences of bishops neglecting notorious abuses:

> God will come; he will not tarry long away. He will come upon such a day as we nothing look for him, and at such an hour as we know not. He will come and cut us in pieces. He will reward us as he does, the hypocrites. He will set us where wailing shall be, my brethren—where gnashing of teeth shall be, my brethren. These be the delicate dishes prepared for the world's well-beloved children. These be the wafers and junkets provided for worldly prelates, wailing and gnashing of teeth. You see, brethren, what sorrow and punishment is provided for you if you be worldlings. If you will not then be vexed, be not the children of the world. If you will not be the children of the world, be not stricken with the love of worldly things; lean not upon them. If you will not die eternally, live not worldly. Come, go to; leave the love of your profit; study for the glory and profit of Christ; seek in your consultations, such things as pertain to Christ, and bring forth at last somewhat that may please Christ. Feed you tenderly with all diligence the flock of Christ. Preach truly the Word of God. Love the light, walk in the light, and so be you the children of light while you are in this world,

that you may shine in the world to come bright as the
stars, with the Father, Son, and Holy Spirit.[45]

In 1537, we find Bishop Latimer placed on the Commission of
Divines, for the publication of a book to set forth the truth of
religion, the result of which commission was *the institution of
a Christian man*. The same year we find him putting forth
some injunctions to the prior of Worcester convent, a
monastic house not yet dissolved, in which among other
things, he commands the prior to have a whole Bible in
English, chained in the church. He orders every member of
the convent to get himself an English New Testament; he
directs a lecture of Scripture to be read in the convent every
day, and Scripture to be read at dinner and supper. Shortly
afterward, he published injunctions to the clergy of his
diocese, in which he commands every one of them to provide
himself with a whole Bible, or at any rate, with a New
Testament, and every day to read over and study one chapter
at the least. He also forbids them to set aside preaching for
any manner of observance, ceremonies, or processions, and
enjoins them to instruct the children in their respective
parishes. All these little facts are deeply instructive. They
show us what an Augaean stable an English diocese was in
Henry the Eighth's day, and what enormous difficulties a
reforming bishop had to overcome.

---

[45] Latimer, *Works,* I, 50.

In 1538, we find Latimer pleading with Lord Cromwell, that Great Malvern Abbey might not be entirely suppressed. He suggests that it should be kept up, "not for monkery," which he says, "God forbid," but "to maintain teaching, preaching, study, and prayer;" and he asks whether it would not be good policy to have two or three of the old monastic houses in every county set apart for such purposes. This was a very wise design, and shows great foresight of the country's wants. Had it been carried into effect, Durham, St. Bees, Lampeter, and King's College would have been unnecessary. The rapacity of Henry the Eighth's courtiers, who had an amazing appetite for the property of the suppressed abbeys, made the suggestion useless.

Compelled to resign

In 1539, Bishop Latimer's episcopate was brought to an end by the enactment of the six Articles already referred to, in which some of the leading tenets of Romanism were authoritatively maintained. He strenuously withstood the passing of this Act, in opposition to the king and the parliament, and the result was that he was compelled to resign his bishopric. It is related, that on the day when this happened, when he came back from the House of Lords to his lodgings, he threw off his robes, and leaping up, declared to those who stood about him, that he found himself lighter than he had been for some time.

The next eight years of Latimer's life appear to have passed away in forced silence, and in retirement. We read little of anything that he did. We do not exactly know where he spent his time, and whether he returned to his old living at West Kington or not. The probability is, that he was regarded as a dangerous and suspected man, and had much difficulty in preserving his life. The only certain fact we know is, that he was at length committed to prison as a heretic, and spent the last year of Henry the Eighth's reign in confinement in the Tower.

Edward VI

When Edward VI came to the throne in 1547, Latimer was at once released from prison, and treated with every mark of respect. His old bishopric of Worcester was offered to him, and the House of Commons presented an address to the Protector Somerset, earnestly requesting that he might be re-appointed. Old age, and increasing infirmities made Latimer decline the proffered dignity and he spent the next six years of his life without any office, but certainly not as an idle man. His chief residence, during these six years, was with his old friend and ally, Archbishop Cranmer, under the hospitable roof of Lambeth Palace. While here, he took an active part in all the measures adopted for carrying forward the Protestant Reformation. He assisted Cranmer in composing the first book of Homilies, and was also one of the divines appointed to reform the Ecclesiastical Law, a work which was never completed. All this time he generally preached twice every Sunday. In the former part of Edward the Sixth's reign he preached constantly before the king. In the latter part, he went to and fro in the midland counties of England, preaching wherever his services seemed to be most wanted, and especially in Lincolnshire. This was perhaps the most useful period of his life. No one of the Reformers, probably, sowed the seeds of sound Protestant doctrine so widely and effectually among the middle classes, as Latimer. The late Mr. Southey bears testimony to this: he says, "Latimer, more than any other man, promoted the Reformation by his preaching."[46]

Sufferings under Bloody Mary

The untimely death of Edward VI and the accession of Queen Mary to the throne in 1553, put an end to Latimer's active exertions on behalf of the Gospel. From that time on he was called to glorify Christ by suffering, and not by doing.

One of the first acts of Mary's government was the apprehension of the leading English Reformers, and Latimer was among the first for whom a warrant was issued. The queen's messenger found him doing his Master's work, as a preacher in Warwickshire, but quite prepared for prison. He had received notice of what was coming six hours before the messenger arrived, from a good man named Careless, and might easily have escaped. But he refused to avail himself of the opportunity. He said: "I go as willingly to London at this present, being called by my Prince to render a reckoning of

---

[46] Robert Southey, *Book of the Church*, II, (Boston: Wells and Lily, 1825), 38.

my doctrine, as ever I went to any place in the world. And I do not doubt but that God, as he has made me worthy to preach his Word to two excellent princes, so he will enable me to witness the same unto the third."

In this spirit he rode cheerfully up to London, and said, as he passed through Smithfield, where heretics were generally burned, "Smithfield has long groaned for me."

Latimer was at once committed to the Tower, in company with Cranmer, Ridley, and Bradford, and for lack of room, all the four were confined in one chamber. There these four martyrs, to use old Latimer's words, "did together read over the New Testament with great deliberation, and painful study,"[47] and unanimously agreed that transubstantiation was not to be found in it. From the Tower, the three bishops were removed to Oxford, in 1554, and there, in 1555, Latimer and Ridley were burned alive at the stake, as obstinate heretics.

Latimer's conduct in prison was answerable to his previous life. For two long years he never lost his spirits, and his faith and patience never failed him. Much of his time was spent in reading the Bible. He says himself, "I read the New Testament over seven times while I was in prison." Much of his time was spent in prayer. Augustine Bernher, his faithful servant, tells us that he often continued kneeling so long that he was not able to get up from his knees without help. Three things he used especially to mention in his prayers at this time. One was, that as God had appointed him to be a preacher and

---

[47] Latimer, *Works*, II, 259.

professor of his Word, so he would give him grace to stand to His doctrine till his death. Another was, that God would of His mercy restore the Gospel of Christ to the realm once again: he often repeated these two words, "once again." The third was, that God would preserve the Princess Elizabeth, and make her a comfort to England. It is a striking fact that all these three prayers were fully granted.

Latimer's conduct at his various trials and examinations before his Popish persecutors was in some respects wiser and better than that of the other martyrs. He knew well enough that his death was determined on, and he was quite right. Gardiner, the Popish Bishop of Winchester, had said openly, that "he would have the ax laid at the root of the tree: the bishops and most powerful preachers ought certainly to die." Bonner, the Popish Bishop of London had said, "God do so to Bonner, and more also, if one of the heretics escape me." Acting on this impression, Latimer told Ridley before the trial, that he should say little. "They talk of free disputation," said he, "but their argument will be as it was with their forefathers, 'We have a law, and by our law he ought to die.'" Acting on this impression, he did little at his various trials but make a simple profession of his faith. He refused to be led away into lengthy discussions about the opinions of the Fathers, like Cranmer and Ridley. He told his judges plainly, that "the Fathers might be deceived in some points," and that he only "believed them when they said true, and had Scripture with them!" A wiser and truer remark about the Fathers was probably never made.

The death of old Latimer is so beautifully described by Foxe, that I cannot do better than give you the account as nearly as possible in his words. I certainly shall not try to spoil it by any additions of my own, though lack of time will oblige me to abridge it considerably:

The place appointed for the execution was on the north side of Oxford, in the ditch over against Balliol College. For fear of any tumult that might arise to prevent their burning, Lord Williams and the householder of the city, were commanded by the Queen's letter to be assistant, sufficiently armed, and when all things were in readiness, the prisoners were brought forth together, on the 16th of October, 1555.

Ridley came first, in a furred black gown, such as he was accustomed to wear as a bishop. After him came Latimer, in a poor Bristol frieze frock, all worn, with his buttoned cap and a handkerchief over his head, and a long new shroud hanging over his hose, down to his feet.

Ridley, looking back, saw Latimer coming after, to whom he said, "Oh! are you there?" "Yea," said Master Latimer, "as fast as I can follow." At length they came to the stake, one after the other. Ridley first entered the place, and earnestly holding up both his hands looked toward heaven. Shortly after, seeing Latimer, he ran to him, embraced and kissed him, saying, "Be of good cheer, brother, for God will either assuage the fury of the flames, or else strengthen us to abide it."

With that he went to the stake, kneeled down by it, kissed it, and prayed; and behind him Latimer kneeled, earnestly calling upon God. After they arose, one talked with another a little while, but what they said, no one could tell Foxe.[48]

Then were they compelled to listen to a sermon preached by a renegade priest, named Smith, upon the text, "Though I give my body to be burned, and have not charity, I am nothing." They attempted to answer the false statements of this miserable discourse, but were not allowed. Ridley said, "Well I then I commit our cause to Almighty God, who shall impartially judge all." Latimer added his own verse, "Well! there is nothing hid, but it shall be made manifest," and said, "He could answer Smith well enough, if he might be suffered."

They were commanded after this to make ready immediately, and obeyed with all meekness. Ridley gave his clothes, and such things as he had about him to those that stood by, and happy was he that could get any rag of him. Latimer gave nothing, but quietly suffered his keeper to pull off his hose and his other apparel, which was very simple. And now, being stripped to his shroud, he seemed as comely a person

---

[48] Original: said, Foxe could not learn of any man.

to them that stood by as one could desire to see. And though in his clothes he appeared a withered, crooked old man, he now stood quite upright.

Then the smith took a chain of iron, and fastened it about both Ridley's and Latimer's middles to one stake. As he was knocking in a staple, Ridley took the chain in his hands, and said to the smith, "Goodfellow, knock it in hard, for flesh will have its course." A bag of gunpowder was tied about the neck of each. Small sticks[49] were piled round them, and the horrible preparations were completed.

Then they brought a stick[50] kindled with fire, and laid it down at Ridley's feet. To whom Latimer then spoke in this manner, "Be of good comfort, brother Ridley, and play the man; we shall this day light such a candle, by God's grace, in England, as I trust never shall be put out."

And so the fire being kindled, when Ridley saw the fire flaming up toward him, he cried with a loud voice, "Lord, into your hands I commend my spirit; Lord, receive my spirit" and repeated the latter part often. Latimer, crying as vehemently on the other side of the stake, "Father of heaven, receive my soul," received the flame as if embracing it. After he had stroked his face with his hands, and as it were,

---

[49] Original: Faggots.
[50] Original: faggot.

bathed them a little in the fire, he soon died, as it appeared, with very little pain."[51]

And thus much, says Foxe, concerning the end of this old blessed servant of God, Bishop Latimer, for whose "laborious services, fruitful life, and constant death, the whole realm has cause to give great thanks to Almighty God."

And now it is high time for me to turn from the subject of Latimer's life. I have given you a brief sketch of his history from his birth to his death. You will easily believe that for lack of time I have left many things untold. I might dwell on the good man's preaching.

Latimer's preaching

Few probably, have ever addressed an English congregation with more effect than he did. No doubt his sermons that still exist in print,[52] would not suit modern taste. They contain many quaint, odd, and coarse things. They are very familiar, rambling, and long-winded,[53] and often full of gossiping stories. But, after all, we are poor judges in these days, of what a sermon ought to be. A modern sermon is too often a dull, tame, pointless, religious essay, full of measured round sentences, Johnsonian English, bald platitudes, timid statements, and elaborately concocted milk and water. It is a leaden sword, without either point or edge, a heavy weapon,

---

[51] See *Fox's Book of Martyrs*, III, 490–493.
[52] Original: sermons now extant, would not.
[53] Original: and discursive.

and little likely to do much execution. But if a combination of sound Gospel doctrine, plain Saxon language, boldness, liveliness, directness, and simplicity, can make a preacher, few, I suspect, have ever equaled old Latimer.

Courage and faithfulness

I might tell you of the many proofs he gave of courage and faithfulness as a minister. He did not shrink from attacking anybody's sins, even if they were the sins of a king. When Henry VIII checked the diffusion of the Bible, Latimer wrote him a plain-spoken letter, long before he was a bishop, remonstrating with him on his conduct. He feared God, and nothing else did he fear. "Latimer, Latimer," he exclaimed, at the beginning of one of his sermons, "You are going to speak before the high and mighty King Henry VIII, who is able, if he think fit, to take your life away. Be careful what you say. But, Latimer, Latimer, remember also you are about to speak before the King of kings, and Lord of lords. Take heed that you do not displease him."

Unworldliness

I might speak of his unworldliness. He gave up a rich bishopric, and retired into private life, for conscience-sake, without a murmur. He refused that same bishopric again, because he felt too old to fulfill its duties, when he might have had it by saying "Yes." I might speak of his genuine kindliness of heart. He was always the friend of the poor and distressed. Much of his time, while he stayed at Lambeth, was occupied in examining into the cases of people who applied to him for help. I might speak of his diligence. To the very end of his life he used to rise at two o'clock in the morning, and begin reading and study. All this, and much more, I might tell you, but time would fail if I entered into more particulars.

Latimer's Legacy

I trust however, I have given you facts enough to supply you with some faint idea of what the man was. I trust you are ready to agree with me, that he was one of the best bishops this country has ever had, and that it would have been well for the Church of England, if more of her bishops had been like Bishop Latimer, and fewer like Archbishop Laud.

Do not forget, as you think over the history of his life, that he is a glorious instance of the miracles which the grace of God can work. The Spirit can take a fierce Papist, you see, and make him a faithful Protestant. Where the hand of the Lord is, nothing is impossible. Never think that any friend, relation, or companion is too much opposed to the Gospel to become a true Christian. Away with the idea! There are no hopeless cases under the Gospel. Remember Latimer, and never despair.

Do not forget, as you think over Latimer's last days, that he is a glorious proof that Jesus can sustain his people even in the fire, and will be a present help to those who trust Him in their time of need. Think not for a moment that anything is too hard to be borne, if God be with you. Do not give up religion because you see fiery trials in your way, because your place is unfavourable, and circumstances are against you. Remember old Latimer at the stake, and never be cast down.

3

LATIMER'S OPINIONS

The third and last thing which I proposed to do in this work, is[54] to give you a brief account of some of Latimer's opinions.

I ask your special attention to this portion of the book.[55] The circumstances of the times you live in, invest the subject with more than ordinary importance.

You live in days when very strange statements are made in some quarters as to the true doctrines of the Church of England. You live in days, when semi-Popish views about the rule of faith, about justification, about regeneration, about the sacraments, about preaching, are urged upon the attention of Young England, and when the advocates and teachers of these views are coolly arrogating to themselves the credit of being the only sound churchmen.

It is to no purpose that those who repudiate these semi-Popish views, challenge their advocates to prove them by Scripture. The ready answer is at once given, that, whether

---

[54] Original: tonight, was.
[55] Original: the evening's lecture.

these views are Scriptural or not, there can be no doubt they are "church views." It is to no purpose that we deny these views are to be found in the Articles, Liturgy, and Homilies of the Church of England, when honestly and consistently interpreted. We are quietly told that we know nothing about the matter. We are stupid. We are dense. We are blind. We are ignorant. We do not understand plain English. They are the true men. Their views are the true "church views," and if we disagree with them, we must be quite wrong. In short, we are left to infer that, if we are honest and consistent, we ought to leave our dear old church, and give it up to them. I appeal to the experience of many here present. You know well I am describing things which are going on in every part of the land.

Now, as matters have come to this pass, let us see whether we cannot throw a little light on the subject by looking back to the Sixteenth Century.[56] Let us inquire what were the views of the men who laid the foundations of the Church of England, and are notoriously the fathers of the Articles, Homilies, and Liturgy. Let us put old Latimer into the witness-box, and see what his opinions were upon the points in dispute. An honored member of the Church of England at the period when the doctrines of the Church were first brought into shape and form, a near and dear friend and adviser of Archbishop Cranmer, an assistant in the composition of the first book of Homilies, a bishop whose orthodoxy and soundness were never called in question for a

---

[56] Original: three hundred years.

moment by his contemporaries. If any man knows what a true churchman ought to hold, Bishop Latimer must surely be that man; if his views are not true "church" views, I know not whose are.

Bear with me then, for a few minutes, while I give you some extracts from Latimer's works. Bear with me while I try to confirm your minds on the important question of the present day, who is, and who is not, a true churchman?

Scripture

First of all, what did Bishop Latimer think about Scripture? This is a point with which the very existence of true religion is bound up. Some churchmen tell us nowadays, notwithstanding the Sixth Article,[57] that the Bible alone is not the rule of faith, and is not able to make a man wise to salvation. No! it must be the Bible and the fathers, or the Bible and Catholic tradition, or the Bible and the Church, or the Bible explained by the Prayer-book, or the Bible explained by an episcopally-ordained man, but not the Bible alone. Now let us hear Bishop Latimer. He says, in a sermon before Edward VI:

---

[57] The Sixth Article States: "Holy Scripture contains all things necessary for salvation. Consequently whatever is not read in Scripture nor can be proved from Scripture cannot be demanded from any person to believe it as an article of the faith. Nor is any such thing to be thought necessary or required for salvation. By holy Scripture is meant those canonical books of the Old and New Testaments whose authority has never been doubted within the church."

I will tell you what a bishop of this realm once said to me. He sent for me, and marveled that I would not consent to such traditions as were set out. And I answered him, that I would be ruled by God's Book, and rather than depart one jot from it, I would be torn by wild horses. I chanced in our communication, to name the Lord's Supper. "Tush!" says the bishop, "What do you call the Lord's Supper? What new term is this?" There stood by him one Dr. Dubber. He dubbed him by-and-by, and said that this term was seldom read in the doctors. And I made answer, that I would rather follow Paul in using his terms than them, though they had all the doctors on their side.[58]

He says again, in his Conference with Ridley:

A layman, fearing God, is much more fit to understand holy Scripture, than any arrogant or proud priest, yes, than the bishop himself, be he ever so great and glistering in his pontificals. But what is to be said of the Fathers? How are they to be esteemed? St. Augustine answers, giving his rule, that we should not therefore think it true because they say so, do they never so much exceed in holiness and learning, but if they be able to prove their saying by canonical Scripture, or by-good probable reasons; meaning that to be a probable reason, I think, which does orderly follow upon a

---

[58] Latimer, *Works,* I, 121.

right collection and gathering out of the holy Scriptures.

Let the Papists go with their long faith. Be you contented with the short faith of the saints, which is revealed to us in the Word of God written. Adieu to all Popish fantasies. Amen! For one man, having the Scripture, and good reason for him, is more to be esteemed himself alone, than a thousand such as they, either gathered together, or succeeding one another. The Fathers have both herbs and weeds, and Papists commonly gather the weeds and leave the herbs.[59]

I make no comment on these passages, they speak for themselves.

Justification by faith

In the next place, what did Bishop Latimer think about justification by faith? This is the doctrine which Luther truly called the criterion of a standing or falling church. This is the doctrine which, in spite of the Eleventh Article[60] of our Church, many are now trying to obscure, by mingling up with it baptism, the Lord's Supper, our own works, and I don't

---

[59] *The Works of Bishop Ridley*, 114.

[60] The Eleventh Article States: "We are accounted righteous before God solely on account of the merit of our Lord and Saviour Jesus Christ through faith and not on account of our own good works or of what we deserve. Consequently the teaching that we are justified by faith alone is a most wholesome and comforting doctrine. This is taught more fully in the homily on Justification."

know what else.[61] Now let us hear Bishop Latimer. He says, in a sermon preached at Grimsthorpe:

> Christ reputes all those for just, holy, and acceptable before God, which believe in him, which put their trust, hope, and confidence in him. By his passion which he suffered, he merited, that as many as believe in him shall be as well justified by him, as though they had never done any sin, and as though they had fulfilled the law to the uttermost. For we without him are under the curse of the law. The law condemns us. The law is not able to help us. And yet the imperfection is not in the law, but in us. The law itself is holy and good,[62] but we are not able to keep it, and so the law condemns us. But Christ, with his death has delivered us from the curse of the law.[63] He has set us at liberty, and promised that when we believe in him we shall not perish,[64] the law shall not condemn us.[65] Therefore, let us study to believe in Christ. Let us put all our hope, trust, and confidence only in him. Let us patch him with nothing, for, as I told you before, our merits are not able to deserve everlasting life. It is too precious a thing to be merited by man. It is his doing only. God has given

---

[61] Original: I know not what besides.
[62] Romans 7:12.
[63] Galatians 3:13.
[64] John 3:16.
[65] Romans 8:1.

him to us to be our deliverer, and to give us everlasting life.[66]

He says again, in another sermon:

Learn to abhor this most detestable and dangerous poison of the Papists, which go about to thrust Christ out of his office. Learn, I say, to leave all Papistry, and to stick only to the Word of God, which teaches that Christ is not only a judge, but a justifier, a giver of salvation, and a taker away of sin. He purchased our salvation through his painful death, and we receive the same through believing in him, as St. Paul teaches us, "freely you are justified through faith" (Rom. 3:24). In these words of St. Paul, all merits and estimation of works are excluded and clean taken away. For if it were for our works' sake, then it were not freely, but St. Paul said freely. Whether will you now believe, St. Paul, or the Papists?[67]

He says again, in another sermon:

Christ only, and no man else, merited remission, justification, and eternal felicity, for as many as will believe the same. They that will not believe it, shall not have it; for it is no more, but believe and have.[68]

---

[66] Latimer, *Works,* II, 125.
[67] Latimer, *Works,* II, 147.
[68] Latimer, *Works,* I, 421.

Once more, I say these passages require no comment of mine. They speak for themselves.

Regeneration

In the next place, what did Bishop Latimer think about regeneration? This, as you are all aware, is the subject of one of the great controversies of the day. Multitudes of church men, in spite of the Seventeenth Article,[69] and the Homily for Whit-Sunday, maintain that all baptized persons are

---

[69] The Seventeenth Article States: "Predestination to life is the eternal purpose of God, whereby (before the foundations of the world were laid) he has consistently decreed by his counsel which is hidden from us to deliver from curse and damnation those whom he has chosen in Christ out of mankind and to bring them through Christ to eternal salvation as vessels made for honour. Hence those granted such an excellent benefit by God are called according to God's purpose by his Spirit working at the appropriate time. By grace they obey the calling; they are freely justified, and made sons of God by adoption, are made like the image of his only-begotten Son Jesus Christ, they walk faithfully in good works and at the last by God's mercy attain eternal happiness. The reverent consideration of this subject of predestination and of our election in Christ is full of sweet, pleasant and inexpressible comfort to the godly and to those who feel within themselves the working of the Spirit of Christ, putting to death the deeds of the sinful and earthly nature and lifting their minds up to high and heavenly consideration establishes and confirms their belief in the eternal salvation to be enjoyed through Christ and kindles a fervent love towards God. But for inquisitive and unspiritual persons who lack the Spirit of Christ to have the sentence of God's predestination continually before their eyes is a dangerous snare which the Devil uses to drive them either into desperation or into recklessly immoral living (a state no less perilous than desperation). Furthermore we need to receive God's promises in the manner in which they are generally set out to us in holy Scripture, and in our actions we need to follow that will of God which is clearly declared to us in the Word of God."

necessarily regenerate, and receive grace, and the Holy Spirit, at the moment they are baptized. In a word, they tell us that every man, woman, and child, who has received baptism, has also received regeneration, and that every congregation in the Church of England should be addressed as an assembly of regenerated persons. Now let us hear Bishop Latimer. He says, in a sermon preached in Lincolnshire:

> There be two manners of men. Some there be that be not justified, not regenerate, not yet in the state of salvation, that is to say, not God's servants. They lack the renovation, or regeneration. They be not yet come to Christ.[70]

He says, in a sermon preached before Edward VI:

> Christ says, "Except a man be born from above, he cannot see the kingdom of God" (John 3:3). He must have a regeneration. And what is this regeneration? It is not to be christened in water, as those firebrands expound it, and nothing else. How is it to be expounded, then? St. Peter shows that one place of Scripture declares another. It is the circumstance and collection of places that makes Scripture plain. We be born again, says Peter, and how? Not by a mortal seed, but an immortal. What is the immortal seed? By the Word of the living God—by the Word of God preached and opened. Thus comes in our new birth.[71]

---

[70] Latimer, *Works,* II, 7.
[71] Latimer, *Works,* I, 202.

He says, in another Lincolnshire sermon:

> Preaching is God's instrument, whereby he works
> faith in our hearts. Our Saviour says to Nicodemus,
> "Except a man be born anew, he cannot see the
> kingdom of God" (John 3:3). But how comes this
> regeneration? By hearing and believing the Word of
> God, for so says St. Peter.[72]

Once more, I say, these passages require no comment of mine.
They speak for themselves.

The Lord's Supper

In the next place, what did Bishop Latimer think about the
Lord's Supper? This, I need hardly say, is a subject about
which very unprotestant doctrine is often taught in the
present day. Some around us, in the face of the Twenty-
Eighth Article,[73] speak of this sacrament in such a manner,

---

[72] Latimer, *Works,* I, 471.

[73] The Twenty-Eighth Article States: "The Supper of the Lord is
not only a sign of the love that Christians ought to have among themselves
one to another; but rather it is a Sacrament of our Redemption by Christ's
death: insomuch that to such as rightly, worthily, and with faith, receive
the same, the Bread which we break is a partaking of the Body of Christ;
and likewise the Cup of Blessing is a partaking of the Blood of Christ.
Transubstantiation (or the change of the substance of Bread and Wine) in
the Supper of the Lord, cannot be proved by holy Writ; but is repugnant
to the plain words of Scripture, overthroweth the nature of a Sacrament,
and hath given occasion to many superstitions. The Body of Christ is
given, taken, and eaten, in the Supper, only after an heavenly and spiritual
manner. And the mean whereby the Body of Christ is received and eaten

that it is hard to see the difference between their doctrine and Popish transubstantiation, or the sacrifice of the mass. Now let us hear Bishop Latimer. He says in his disputation at Oxford:

> In the sacrament there is none other presence of Christ required than a spiritual presence. And this presence is sufficient for a Christian man, as the presence by which we abide in Christ, and Christ in us, to the obtaining of eternal life, if we persevere in the true Gospel. And this same presence may be called a real presence, because, to the faithful believer, there is the real and spiritual body of Christ.[74]

He says, in the same disputation:

> Christ spoke never a word of sacrificing, or saying of mass; nor promised the hearers any reward but among the idolaters, with the devil and his angels, except they repent speedily. Therefore, sacrificing priests should now cease forever; for now all men ought to offer their own bodies a quick sacrifice, holy and acceptable before God.[75] The supper of the Lord was instituted to provoke us to thanksgiving, and to

in the Supper is Faith. The Sacrament of the Lord's Supper was not by Christ's ordinance reserved, carried about, lifted up, or worshipped."

[74] Latimer, *Works,* II, 252.

[75] Romans 12:1.

stir us up by preaching of the Gospel, to remember[76] his death till he comes again.[77]

He says, in his last examination:

There is a change in the bread and wine, and such a change as no power but the omnipotence of God can make, in that which before was bread should now have the dignity to exhibit Christ's body. And yet the bread is still bread, and the wine still wine. For the change is not in the nature, but the dignity.[78]

He says, in one of his Lincolnshire sermons:

Whosoever eats the mystical bread, and drinks the mystical wine worthily, according to the ordinance of Christ, he receives surely the very body and blood of Christ spiritually, as it shall be most comfortable to his soul. He eats with the mouth of his soul, and digests with the stomach of his soul, the body of Christ. And, to be short, whosoever believes in Christ, puts his hope, trust, and confidence in him, he eats and drinks him. For the spiritual eating is the right eating to eternal life, not the corporeal eating.[79]

---

[76] 1 Corinthians 11:26.
[77] Latimer, *Works,* II, 256.
[78] Latimer, *Works,* II, 286.
[79] Latimer, *Works,* I, 459.

It would be easy to multiply quotations of this kind to an endless length, if time permitted. There is hardly a controverted subject in the present day on which I could not give you some plain, Scriptural, sensible, sound opinion of Bishop Latimer.

Preaching

Would you like to know what he thought about preaching? Did he think little of it, as some do in this day, and regard it as a means of grace very subordinate to sacraments and services? No! indeed he did not. He calls it "the office of salvation, and the office of regeneration." He says, "Take away preaching, and take away salvation." He says, "This office of preaching is the only ordinary way that God has appointed to save us all. Let us maintain this, for I know none other." He declares that:

> preaching is the thing the devil wrestled most against. It has been all his study to decay this office. He works against it as much as he can. He has made unpreaching prelates, and stirred them up by heaps to persecute this office in the title of heresy.[80]

---

[80] Latimer, *Works,* I, 155; 203; 306; 349; 202.

Ceremonies and candles

Would you like to hear what he thought about a gorgeous ceremonial and candles in churches? He says plainly, that these things come from the devil:

> Where the devil is resident, and has his plow going, there away with book, and up with candles; away with Bible, and up with beads; away with the light of the Gospel, and up with the light of candles, yea, even at noon-day. Where the devil is resident that he may prevail, up with all superstition and idolatry, censing, painting of images, candles, palms, ashes, holy water, and new services of man's inventing.[81]

Unity

Would you like to know what he thought about unity? Did he think, as some do now, that it is the one thing needful, and that we should give up everything in order to obtain it? No! indeed. He says:

> Unity must be according to God's holy Word, or else it were better war than peace. We ought never to regard unity so much that we forsake God's Word for her sake.[82]

The foreign Reformers

Would you like to know what he thought about the foreign Reformers? Did he lightly esteem them, as some do nowadays,

---

[81] Latimer, *Works,* I, 71.
[82] Latimer, *Works,* I, 487.

because they did not retain episcopacy? No! indeed he did not. He says:

> I heard say, Melanchthon, that great clerk, should come here. I would wish him, and such as he is, to have two hundred pounds a year. The king would never want it. There is yet among us two great learned men, Peter Martyr and Bernard Ochin, which have a hundred marks a piece. I would the king would bestow a thousand pounds on that sort.[83]

Councils and convocations

Would you like to know what he thought about councils and convocations? Did he regard them as the grand cure-all[84] for all ecclesiastical evils, like those around us, whose cry is, "Give us synodical action, or we die?" He says to Ridley:

> touching councils and convocations, I refer you to your own experience to think of our own country's parliaments and convocations. The more part in my time did bring forth the Six Articles. Afterward the more part did repeal the same. The same Articles are now again restored. Oh! What uncertainty is this.[85]

---

[83] Latimer, *Works,* I, 141.
[84] Original: grand panacea.
[85] Ridley, *Works,* 130.

And he says, in another place:

> More credence is to be given to one man having the holy Word of God for him, than to ten thousand without the Word. If it agrees with God's Word it is to be received. If it agrees not, it is not to be received, though a council had determined it.[86]

Protestant preaching

Would you like to know what he thought of thorough-going Protestant preaching? Did he think, as some do now, that if a sermon contains a good deal of truth, a little false doctrine may be excused and allowed? No! indeed he did not. He says:

> Many preach God's way, and shall preach a very good and godly sermon, but at last they will have a blanched almond, one little piece of Popery patched in to powder their matter with, for their own lucre and glory. They make a mingling of the way of God and man's way, a mingle-mangle, as men serve pigs in my country.[87]

I will not hold you up any longer with these extracts. I have already trespassed too much on your attention. I will only ask you to remember well whose words I have been quoting, and when they were spoken.

---

[86] Latimer, *Works,* I, 288.
[87] Latimer, *Works,* I, 290.

The real opinions of the Church

These words were not spoken last year. They did not fall from the lips of the rectors of St. George's, Bloomsbury; or St. Mary, Whitechapel; or St. George's, Southwark. They were not spoken by the ministers of Park Chapel, Chelsea; or of Portman Chapel; or the Lock; or St. John's, Bedford-row, or by some platform-orator, at Exeter Hall. No! Gentlemen, the words I have quoted are from the 16th Century.[88] They are the words of one of the best bishops the Church of England ever had. They are the words of the man who helped to compose our first book of Homilies. They are the words of the friend and adviser of Archbishop Cranmer. They are the words of one whom king and parliament delighted to honor.

Why was the speaker of these words not cast out of the church? Why was he not reprimanded? Why was he not reviled as a man of low, unchurchmanlike opinions? Why was he not proceeded against, and persecuted for his views? How is it that he was persecuted only by Papists, but always honored by Protestants—persecuted by Bonner, Gardiner, and Bloody Mary; but honored by Cranmer, Ridley, and Edward VI?

I will give you a plain answer to these questions. I answer them by saying that, in the Sixteenth Century,[89] no man in his senses doubted that Latimer's opinions were the real opinions of the Church of England. I go on further to affirm,

---

[88] Original: are three hundred years old.
[89] Original: that, three hundred years ago.

that the truest and best members of the Church of England at the present day, are those whose views are most in harmony with those of good Bishop Latimer. And I say that, to tell men who love the Church of England with deep affection, that they are not sound churchmen, merely because they agree with Latimer and not with Laud, is to bring against them a most unfair and unwarrantable charge.

Be Protestant and Evangelical

And now let me conclude this book[90] with three practical remarks.

For one thing, let me advise the members of the Church of England Young Men's Society, to take care that their Society never departs from its declared principles. Sound principles are the roots of a Society's success. Without these, your means and appliances for doing good will prove comparatively useless. Your libraries, and reading-rooms, and lectures, will fail to confer on you lasting benefits. Without sound principles, they may look well in your annual reports; but, like a tree rotten at the root, they will bring no fruit to perfection.

Take up your stand boldly on the principle of the English Reformers. Never shrink from avowing yourselves to be a thoroughly Protestant and evangelical body. Do not be shy of those two words. Such avowal may lose you the support of a few pretended friends, who will drop off like leaves in autumn

---

[90] Original: this lecture.

when they see your decision. It will, however, strengthen you in the long run, and make you an evergreen tree. Pardon the freedom of this hint. I give it because you live in evil days, and because I am anxious you should hoist the right colors, and be an unmistakable Society.

In the next place, let me earnestly exhort you, as individuals, never to be ashamed of holding what are called evangelical views within the Church of England. Listen not to those supercilious gentlemen, on the one side, who would have you believe that if you are not high churchmen, like themselves, you are no churchmen at all. Listen not to those exceedingly kind friends, on the other side, who try to persuade you that the Established Church is a regular Popish concern, and ought to be left at once. Both these are ancient tricks. Against both these tricks be on your guard.

Do not be bullied out of the Church of England by the high churchman's assertion that you are only a tolerated party, and have no business by his side. No doubt you live in a communion where great freedom of opinion is allowed. But to tell men of evangelical views that they are merely tolerated, is a downright insult to the memory of the Reformers. Let us make answer to people who tell us so that if they have forgotten Latimer and the 16th Century,[91] we have not. Let us say that we are not going to desert the church of Latimer, in order to please men who wish to lord it over God's heritage, and have things all their own way. Sure I am that, if might

---

[91] Original: and three hundred years ago.

should ever prevail over right, and the friendship of Latimer should be thrust out of the church, by force, and the House of Commons should, be mad enough to sanction it—sure am I, that the men thrust out would be better churchmen than the men left behind.

And do not be wheedled out of the Church by the arguments of men outside, who would probably be glad to be in it, if they only saw the way. When the fox, in an old fable, could not reach the grapes, he said they were sour. When the fox, in another fable, lost his tail in a trap, he tried to persuade his friends that foxes did much better without tails, and advised them to get rid of their own. Do not forget the moral of that fable; do not be enticed into biting off your own tails. Rest assured, that with all its faults and defects, the Church of England has very high privileges to offer to its members. Think well about these privileges. Do not be always poring over the defects. Resolve that you will not lightly cast these privileges away.

Above all, never, never forget that evangelical views are not only theoretically sound and agreeable to the minds of the Reformers, but they are also of vital importance to the very existence of the Church of England. Never has our beloved Church stood so low in this country, as when evangelical views have been at zero, and almost forgotten. Never has she stood so high as when the views of Latimer and the Reformers have been honestly preached, and carried out. So far from being ashamed of evangelical opinions, you may be satisfied that the maintenance of them is rapidly becoming a matter of life or death to your own communion. Take away Latimer's views, and I firmly believe the whole Establishment would collapse before the pressure from without, and come to the ground.

Beware of the Church of Rome

Last of all, let me entreat you all, as Englishmen, to beware of countenancing any retrograde movement in this country toward the Church of Rome, and to resist such movement by every means in your power, from whatever quarter it may come.

I am sure that this warning is one which the times loudly call for. The Church of Rome has risen up among us with renewed strength in the last few years. She does not disguise her hope that England, the lost planet, will soon resume her orbit in the so-called Catholic system, and once more revolve in blind obedience round the center of the Vatican. She has succeeded in blinding the eyes of ignorant persons to her real character. She has succeeded in securing the unexpected aid of misguided men within our own Establishment. A hundred little symptoms around us tell us how real the danger is. Laud and the non-jurors are cried up, Latimer and the Reformers are cried down. Historical works are industriously circulated, in which Bloody Mary is praised, and Protestant Elizabeth blamed. A morbid tenderness toward Romanists, and a virulent bitterness toward Dissenters, have sprung up side by side. An unhealthy attention is paid to what is called medieval taste. Thousands of tracts are sown broad-cast over the land in which the three leading phrases to be seen are generally those three ominous words: priest, catholic and church. The use of the rosary, prayers for the dead, and the Hail Mary, is deliberately recommended to the members of the English Church. Little by little, I fear, the edge of English feeling about Popery is becoming blunt and dull. Surely I have good reason to tell you to beware of the Church of Rome.

Remember the darkness in which Rome kept England when she last had the supreme power. Remember the gross ignorance and degrading superstitions which prevailed in Bishop Latimer's youth. Think not for a moment that these are ancient things, and that Rome is changed. The holy-coat of Tréves, the winking picture at Rimini, the mental enslavement[92] in which unhappy Italy is kept, the notorious practices which go on in the Holy City to this day, are all witnesses that Rome, when she has power, is not changed at all. Remember this, and beware.

Remember the horrible persecutions which Rome carried on against true religion when she last had uncontrolled sway in this country. Remember the atrocities which disgraced the days of Bloody Mary, and the burning of Bishop Latimer. Think not for a moment that Rome is altered. The persecution of Bible readers in Madeira, and the imprisonment of the Madiai, are unmistakable proofs that,

---

[92] Original: thralldom.

after centuries,[93] the old persecuting spirit of Rome still remains as strong as ever. Remember this also, and beware.

Shall we, in the face of such facts as these, return to the bondage in which our forefathers were kept? Shall we give up our Bibles, or be content to sue for sacerdotal license to read them? Shall we submit ourselves humbly to Italian priests? Shall we go back to the adoration of pigs' bones, ducks' blood, and saints' toe nails? God forbid—I say for one—God forbid! Let the dog return to his vomit.[94] Let the sow that was washed, return to her wallowing in the mire. Let the idiotic prisoner go back to his chains. But God forbid that Israel should return to Egypt! God forbid that England should go back into the arms of Rome! God forbid that old Latimer's candle should ever be put out!

Work, every one, if you would prevent such a miserable consummation. Work hard for the extension of pure, Scriptural, and evangelical religion at home and abroad. Labor to spread it among the Jews, among the Roman Catholics, among the heathen. Labor not least to preserve and maintain it, by every constitutional means, in your own church.

Cherish, every one, if you would prevent the increase of Romanism—cherish and cultivate a brotherly feeling toward all orthodox Protestants, by whatever name they may be called. Away with the old rubbishy opinion, that the Church

---

[93] Original: after three hundred years.

[94] Proverbs 26:11.

of England occupies a middle position, a via media between dissent and Rome. Cast it away, for it is false. You might as well talk of the Isle of Wight being midway between England and France. Between us and Rome there is a gulf, and a broad and deep gulf too. Between us and orthodox Protestant dissent, there is but a thin partition wall. Between us and Rome the differences are about essential doctrines, and things absolutely necessary to salvation. Between us and dissent the division is about things indifferent, things in which a man may err, and yet be saved. Rome is a downright open enemy, attacking the very foundation of our religion. Dissent is an ally, and friendly power, not wearing our uniform, nor yet, as we think, so well-equipped as we are, but still an ally, and fighting on the same side. Oh! do not let this hint be thrown away. Cherish, I do beseech you, a kind, brotherly feeling toward all who love the same Saviour, believe the same doctrines, and honor the same Bible as yourselves.

Pray, everyone, if you would prevent the increase of Romanism—pray night and day, that God may preserve this country from Popery, and not deal with it according to its sins. It is a striking fact that almost the last prayer of good King Edward VI on his deathbed, was a prayer to this effect: "O, my Lord God, defend this realm from Papistry, and maintain thy true religion." There was a prayer in the Litany of our Prayer-book, in 1549, which, I think, never ought to have been cast out of it:

From all sedition, and privy conspiracy—from the tyranny of the Bishop of Rome, and all his detestable enormities—from all false doctrine, and heresy—from hardness of heart, and contempt of your word and commandments, Good Lord, deliver us!

To that prayer may you ever be able to say heartily, Amen, and amen!

London, February 28th, 1853.

MATTHEW HENRY

A CHURCH
IN THE HOUSE

Foreword by Joseph C. Harrod

ISBN: 978-1-77526-333-3

Matthew Henry exhorts fathers to lead their homes well in family worship. This is an excellent resource for those who are aiming to be faithful in family discipleship.

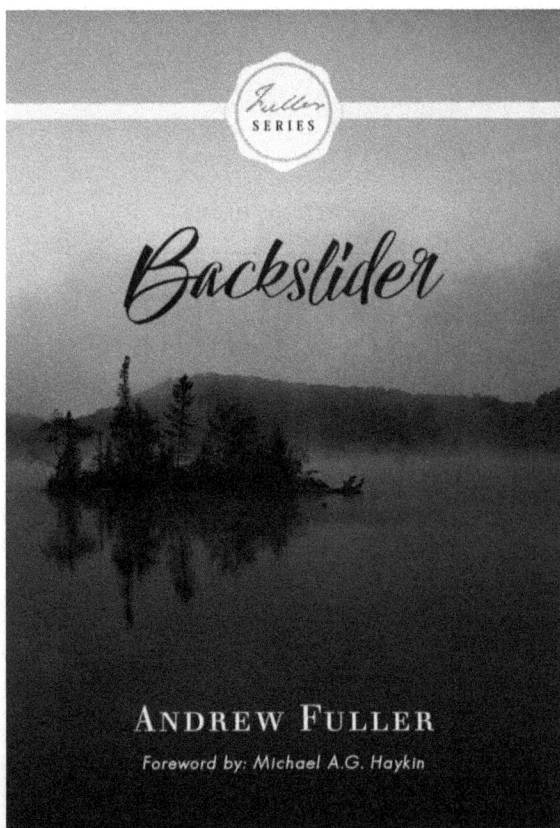

ISBN: 978-1-77526-334-0

Fuller deals with the issue of backsliding: when genuine Christians lose their passion for Christ and his kingdom. This was not a theoretical issue for Fuller, therefore, and his words, weighty when he first wrote them, are still worthy of being pondered—and acted upon.

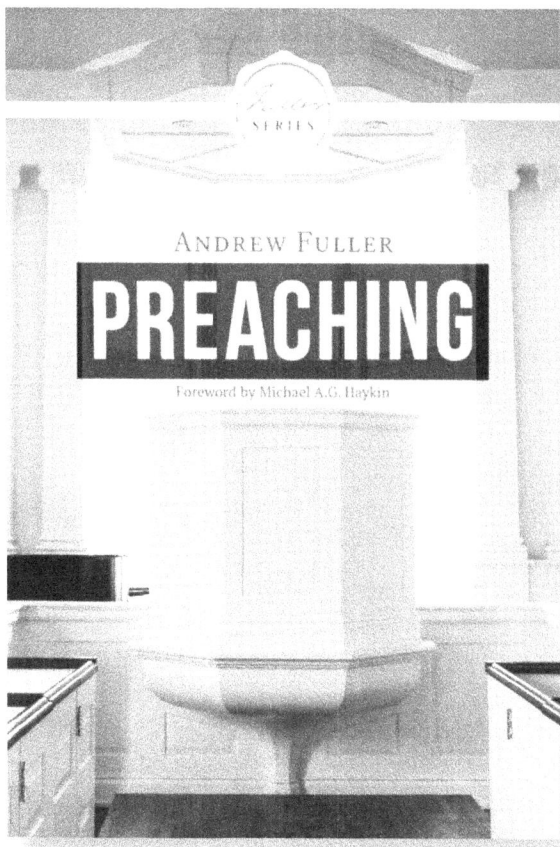

ISBN: 978-1-77526-336-4

Fuller wrote to encourage a young minister in sermon preparation and reading this work will be of great value to any preacher today.

ISBN: 978-1-77526-339-5

In the eyes of Fuller, Samuel Pearce (1766–1799) was the epitome of the spirituality of their community. In fact, in that far-off day of the late eighteenth century Pearce was indeed well known for the anointing that attended his preaching and for the depth of his spirituality. It was said of him that "his ardour … gave him a kind of ubiquity; as a man and a preacher, he was known, he was felt everywhere."

Date Completed	Name

www.ingramcontent.com/pod-product-compliance
Lightning Source LLC
Chambersburg PA
CBHW071623040426

42452CB00009B/1461